THE ST★RS

1002

Quotes by Ankush Modawal

OMNIBUS EDITION

From the Groundbreaking Author of **Black Books**, Blue Book and the *Gold Book*

ANKUSH M★DAWAL

The information contained in this book is intended to be educational and not for diagnosis, prescription, or treatment of any health disorder whatsoever. The information should not replace consultation with a competent healthcare professional. The content of the book is intended to be used as an adjunct to a rational and responsible healthcare program prescribed by a healthcare practitioner. The author is in no way responsible for any misuse of the material.

The intent of the author is only to offer information of a general nature to help you in your quest for emotional and spiritual well-being. In the event you use any of the information in this book for yourself, which is your constitutional right, the author and the publisher assume no responsibility for your actions.

THE ST★R

www.ankushmodawal.com
Copyright ©*Ankush Modawal* 2010

2 Dawns Publishing
WORDS TO LIVE BY
B-125 Mount Kailash, 1st Floor, SFS FLATS, New Delhi 65, India

Books *by* Ankush Modawal

Black Book One

Think Your Dreams to Reality

Genre: Law of Attraction
Released 2008

Black Book II

Lost Ancient Codes of Creating Miracles

Genre: Law of Attraction
Released 2009

Blue Book

MBA MaFia Exposed

Genre: Dark Comic Fiction/Reality
Released 2011

Golden rules of the rich & famous for manifesting money

Genre: Attracting Wealth
Released 11.11.2011

{SMS 2 GOD}

A 1 to 1 with the Universe

Genre: Signs from the Universe/Spiritual Game
Released 12.12.2012

THE ST★R

501

Quotes of Power, Invincibility and Fortune

The Star is dedicated to the sacrifices I made that made me cry because as my tears fell, I rose to become what I had only dreamt of becoming, A Star.

For the one reading this The Star, is dedicated to that one person in your life who inspired the most greatness in you, your Star

"I can't imagine and couldn't even have dreamt of becoming what I am today. Of course that's just a figure of speech that I use because anyone who has ever achieved anything unimaginable imagined it either consciously or unconsciously."

2

"Thinking IT is wanting IT, whatever IT may be."

3

"To all of life's questions, you are the only answer."

4

"Don't try selling something your mind hasn't bought."

5

"Anything spoken often eventually becomes the truth of your life."

6

"A true connoisseur sees a priceless diamond while others see a worthless lump of coal."

7

"The only space you will ever require is the space between your ears."

8

"Every great friend you have right now was once just a stranger to you."

9

"Monkey see, monkey do. Human see, human do!"

10

"God offers nourishment equally to a rose as well as a weed."

11

"Just like food, yesterday's fresh thoughts are today's turd."

12

"Dependence creates victims."

13

"Patience is a virtue of the dead."

14

"You live your truest moments alone."

15

"If it feels like a struggle, you aren't doing it right."

16

"Nothing is too good to be true for the one who dreams."

17

"Gossiping is a symptom of boredom."

18

"Silence is the language of the evolved."

19

"You and God can never have a breakup!"

20

"Any feeling that is not felt mutually in a relationship invariably transforms into pain."

21

"Cynics stack the odds against themselves by bombarding their brains with facts."

22

"BIG things start with baby steps."

23

"Take advice only from those you want to become like."

24

"In the presence of your awareness and the absence of your desire, what you want, manifests."

25

"Your destiny is not written or engraved somewhere as the red lines on your hands because even people with no arms make one."

26

"A book is a man's cheapest best friend."

27

"The movie of your life is too short to have any drama in it."

28

"Some of us are just born to rule this world in spite of the circumstances we were born in."

29

"People will always ask you about how you do the things you do best and you will be unable to explain to them the gifts God gave you."

30

"Nothing changes until you do."

31

"It is we who decide for ourselves how deserving we are."

32

"When you stop trying to make things happen, they'll happen because trying is not the same as being."

33

"When inspiration comes knocking on the doors of your mind, you must divorce all lethargy, sleep and incompetence or else it will leave you for a more hospitable habitat."

34

"All reality is your perception of it."

35

"Being happy is possibly the best possible worship."

36

"Pay heed to the gentle nudges of the Universe before it manifests a situation that will push you hard to grab your attention."

37

"A person who speaks rudely but with a good intent is abhorred more than a person who speaks nicely while harboring ulterior motives."

38

"If you don't wake up with the clear image of what you want to become sooner or later in life, it's best if you stayed in bed!"

39

"Small fishes hang around a big fish to feed off from the scraps it leaves behind, this behavior is often imitated by humans!"

40
"Whenever you look closely, you'll realize that you have everything you need to take the next step."

41
"Forgiveness is the sweetest revenge, because you stop giving your most precious gifts, your time, focus and energy."

42
"No other person knows how precious your tears are because the value of raw diamonds is seldom known."

43
"When you trust yourself, face your fears and take risks, this Universe will become biased towards you."

44
"Get over the false fact that you are not good enough and this Universe will make you realize that you always were!"

45
"You don't lose someone when they die, you lose a part of who you were when they were around."

46

"What do you want? Or, let's rephrase that a bit, what do you choose to be thankful for?"

47

"There is no other better perverted pleasure than doing what others said you couldn't."

48

"When you run behind something, it runs away from you."

49

"If someone is stupid enough to not realize your value, be smart enough to let them go."

"The most crucial mistake people make is that when they give something to someone, they expect the same thing back from that very same person. However, the Universe will always give back to you what you gave out, but not necessarily from that exact same person."

51

"Your life will be valued for the work you have done with and in it."

52

"Like a pig, our mind feasts on everything with equal fervor."

53

"Unconditional love is not only the true nature of God, it is what God is and to practice love is the only humane religion."

54

"Life is not unfair and always delivers to you what you have been asking for or something even better, so if you feel like shit, life will give you the best crap possible!"

55

"Mercilessly remove from your life what you don't like."

56

"If learning the new leads to anything, unlearning the old leads to more."

57

"A world of possibilities awaits not those with great knowledge but for people who apply what they know."

58

"There will always be haters in your life who will be jealous of your successes and it's your duty to constantly keep giving them reasons which pisses them off even more!"

59

"A few dirty crumpled pieces of paper can never make the world go around!"

60

"The best investment advice I can give you is to keep all your eggs in one basket; yourself."

61

"The only way to become 'lucky' is to become a master of your desires and a slave of your intuition."

62

"The positive thing about all negative experiences is that they teach and make us grow the most."

63

"Distance resides in the mind, love lives in the heart."

64

"Choose to love your life more than you hate the people in it."

65

"We started dying the moment we were born but most people go through life as if they are already dead."

66

"Mistaking niceness of others and perceiving it as weakness is one of the biggest blunders that you can ever commit."

67

"If God was a person, she sure as Hell would be fun!"

68

"A man only becomes a monster when he is pushed to his emotional limits, it's not a threat it's a promise."

69

"The secret to live a happy life is choosing to surrender to God rather than being controlled by the Ego."

70

"Most of us have become like robots, repeating what we have been programmed with, without questioning its validity."

71

"People living around you will show what's alive in you."

72

"God uses imperfect people to touch the lives of other imperfect people to make them better."

73

"Nobody grows alone, when you rise in life, you can't help but contribute to the growth of those around you."

74

"A frog should not look at a lizard and say, hey, you're ugly, because he isn't exactly prince charming either!"

75

"We all live in a house but it's the people in it who make it a home."

76

"People don't learn to do as much by learning something than they learn by doing it."

77

"In life, there is a hard way and there is an easy way, and you get to choose which one you take."

78

"A mistake committed by someone costs those who are in emotional and physical proximity to him."

79

"Laughter is more contagious than the diseases it cures."

80

"The stupid thing to do is to hang on to the people who have said their good byes to you."

81

"We are all one-drous, separation is just an illusion for you to enjoy and not to be bound by it."

82

"Never wait and watch to see what happens, see it happen in your mind and then wait to watch it happen!"

83

"A 'no' might mean 'not now' but it seldom means, 'never.'"

84

"Misery might attract pity but never commands respect."

85

"Most people believe that controlling someone means loving them but true love is acceptance and allowing the other person to be, while being with her."

86

"People complain about not having a car and that they have to walk. They should listen to those who don't have legs and feel blessed for what they already have."

87

"All wars are waged on difference of opinions."

88

"True genius is often misunderstood but never misguided."

89

"Just like when you make a shopping list, it's highly unlikely that you'll miss out on whatever's on it, the same rule applies when you write down your goals."

90

"You are allowed to make mistakes, it's alright, everyone makes them, but don't allow them to make you what you don't want to become."

91

"Your mornings are a hint as to how your day will go."

92

"Money manifests in your life and a result of feeling rich."

93

"Be nice to animals and people who piss you off, it's a biological imperative!"

94

"A cornerstone that is based on lies, always crumbles it's building to the ground."

95

"What you are worth will show without you telling about it."

96

"Wealth is impartial to us just like the air we breathe."

97

"People don't cheat on each other, they just have different agendas."

98

"There is no punishment other than the one you inflict upon yourself."

99

"Just like venom is used to create antivenom, use all your rage, hate, jealousy and every other poisonous negative emotion to create something worthwhile with it, that's the way a champion lives."

100

"Be shameless, stubborn and stupid about your dreams! Though the ones around you might hate you for being that way at first for whatever reasons they perceive justified, at the end, you'll love yourself and eventually end up being loved by the whole world."

101

"Most have awesome talent but little belief in what they do, some have little talent and awesome belief in what they do, the latter always win, hands down."

102

"The ones who say that they are smart enough and don't need to read self-help books are really the ones who need to read them the most!"

103

"No matter how crazy, fucked up or stupid your beliefs are, they will all come to pass. Choose to believe things and in things which you would like to experience in your life."

104

"Your parents might have given life to you but they can't take responsibility or be held responsible for it forever."

105

"Ignorance is one of the greatest causes of all suffering and one of the supreme virtues of happiness."

106

"Take everything 'bad' that comes in your life as a blessing and that is what it will eventually become."

107

"People who believe that things are too good to be true will ruin them till the point they believed they were not."

108

"Most become too busy trying to find something that they become too blind to see that it's right in front of them."

109

"On your road to success, when you cut and get in front of others, you are bound to piss them off."

110

"Assumption is positive thinking personified to the creative minds and to the fool, it will be their death."

111

"Choosing the best is not a matter of being able to afford it but a decision to refuse to settle for the mediocre."

112

"Be happy with what you have but never be satisfied because every great invention was caused by dissatisfaction."

113

"Successful people are not only great initiators, but they also finish whatever they start."

114

"The trick to manifesting what you want is to want it badly and not want it at all at the same time!"

115

"Suffering the side effects of cheap medicine is the same as suffering for circumstances created by cheap thoughts."

116

"Your success in any endeavor depends upon discerning two things as early as possible; what works and what doesn't."

117

"Regret is one of the most expensive emotional expenses and senseless spending of life."

118

"A good sense of humor means the ability to laugh at bad jokes when life makes you the butt of them!"

119

"Live a life of non-judgment, and deliberately extend love and acceptance to people no matter how bad you think they are."

120

"A good teacher is a student of the students he teaches because he learns from them what they need to learn from him."

121

"Be sweet to everyone and you'll attract others to you like honey attracts flies."

122

"Be very choosy about the people you hang out with because A LOT depends on it."

123

"The only way to annihilate something is to ignore it and give the gift of attention to its exact opposite."

124

"Not having all the answers to life's questions is what keeps us human and striving to know those answers makes us great."

125

"The things that almost killed you, almost didn't, be grateful."

126

"God speaks to you all the time, you just have to be willing enough to listen to her."

127

"Sometimes it happens that when you give someone your heart, they'll give you the finger!"

128

"I don't fret about my work being appreciated, I just know it will and it does."

129
"Sometimes, I don't know why I do something when my intuition tells me to only to later realize that it was right."

130
"Our thoughts make us what we are and thus every person is a self-thought or a self-made man."

131
"It is never a question of what you are getting back, but it is imperative that you realize what you are giving out."

132
"When you capture someone's heart, you can conquer their mind, body and soul."

133
"Don't expect others to understand your dreams because you are the only one who can see how magnificent they feel to you."

134
"We use our minds like an early man would've used a computer of the 26th century!"

135

"An energy vampire is treated like an intruding mosquito and those who radiate their light are observed in awe like fireflies."

136

"When your best is not enough, let go."

137

"Look forward to looking forward in life."

138

"If you are inspired, nothing can motivate you."

139

"Those who help us in our time of need are rarely forgotten."

140

"One day you won't be here, but the consequences of your deeds will reverberate around those you leave behind."

141

"Reality is what you dream."

142

"People don't fall in love, they rise in it."

143

"A valuable life is invested more in doing for others than spent on itself."

144

"Positivity repels negative people like a mosquito repellant gets rid of mosquitoes!"

145

"If you continue telling horror stories of the past in your life, be sure that a sequel is in the making!"

146

"The relief you get after sneezing is metaphorically the same as and when you release any negativity."

147

"You can choose to suffer for the mistakes of others for your entire life but realize that it's entirely your choice, life and responsibility."

148

"We are destined or doomed to become exactly like our parents depending upon who they were and if we don't do anything about it."

149

"It's easy to love a lovable person, the real challenge for you in life would be to appreciate goodness in the people who have been mean, bad or unfair to you."

150

"Don't judge people based on what they think, say, do or what they have done. You have no idea about the shit they have gone through in life and if you were in their shoes, you probably wouldn't have been able to handle the situation that manifested any better."

151

"The things we think of as a big deal really aren't."

152

"Use your own brain rather than the opinion of others."

153

"Your reality is not what you think IT IS, but IT IS what you think."

154

"When you become the person you aspire to be, you won't think the way you think right now and when you begin to think about the kind of thoughts you will think then, you will start to become the vision of yourself you aspire to be."

155

"Be the best person you can be right now because you only have today."

156

"Your definition of The Best depends upon what you wish to accomplish."

157

"The quickest way to teach others is to live by the
example of what you preach."

158

"Everyone has a different definition of success. Define
what it means to you and take baby steps towards it
every waking hour, every day and if you can do this
sincerely, you will be astonished by the miracles this
Universe will unravel for you."

159

"Short term vision is a shortcut to Hell."

160

"Do all that can be done today and you won't have to
worry about tomorrow."

161

"Explaining something to those who are not ready to
understand is like teaching a rock to speak Chinese!"

162

"When you dissect your thinking, you will discover the viruses of the mind that plague your life and breed on your disappointments."

163

"Ideas have a life of their own."

164

"Confidence is the essential ingredient in making yourself of value."

165

"Don't give a tiny rat's ass about how what you want will come into your life, that's a sure fire way to make it manifest faster!"

166

"No matter how much you coax or coerce someone out of their confused state, unless they commit a mistake that hurts them to their very core, they won't learn."

167

"Life has a way of having its way with us."

168

"What you know matters more than who you know."

169

"Learn to distinguish between the loud blabber of your
ego and the soft whisper of your intuition."

170

"You must become the select few who go against the
herd of people and with the flow of the Universe."

171

"The sun doesn't care who it shines for."

172

"The habits you make or break, make or break you."

173

"Ego is not the same as self-respect and you must
compromise on one of them to truly know the other."

174

"All material possessions are good, until they are used as
the means to an end and not as the end itself."

175

"To get new things done, you must do new things."

176

"No excuse is good enough to validate a life of misery."

177

"Sometimes it takes a swift kick in the ass to make things happen!"

178

"When I am really happy, I like pissing off pissed people by smiling."

179

"Everything we ask for doesn't always come on good time but in God's time."

180

"Those who depend on themselves are depended on by others."

181

"When two hearts keep thinking about each other, God keeps them together."

182

"Everyone thinks what they think is right, even Hitler was right in his own right!"

183

"A difference in attitude about the world makes a world of a difference in your life."

184

"Believe to a point of knowing in a miracle and expect it to happen to have it happen."

185

"Love and God are the two most misunderstood words in the English Dictionary."

186

"Be someone who brings beauty and excitement in the life of all creation that you touch."

187

"How a man becomes after drinking does not depend on the alcohol he is drinking but on the man himself."

188

"Great achievements are not the cause of becoming great, becoming great is the cause of great achievements."

189

"Life changes for the best when you ask yourself the questions you are most afraid to answer."

190

"There is a time to hold on and a time to let go, choose right now, which one is right for you, right now."

191

"Killing your expectations from everyone makes everything you get from them seem like a blessing."

192

"Just like you would be shit scared to fly a Jumbo Jet, the fear of having to handle power is what keeps it away."

193

"Care enough for people only so much so that they begin to take care of themselves and never so much so that they just stop caring for your care and begin to take you for granted."

194

"When you feel lost in the crowd, look at your fingerprints on your fingertips to remind yourself of the fact that there is no one like you ever created and never will be."

195

"There is nothing wrong with you except for the fact that you think there is."

196

"Love almost always is at its highest in the absence of the presence of the one you love."

197

"Keep your dreams to yourself and in the confines of your heart until you believe in them enough to make them manifest, otherwise they might die in the harsh environment of reality."

198

"A little bit of hope held within your heart will manifest something in your life that will aid you to feel a bit more of hope than what you had earlier held in it."

199

"Instead of searching for meaningful relationships, I only live in search of meaningful moments because that's what they are made of."

200

"We feel grateful for things after we get them, but if you thank the Universe for things you want even before you have possession of them, whatever you want HAS to come to you, as surely as a rock dropped from the air will land on the ground."

201
"Learn to become all that you will ever need."

202
"It's easy to attain something but the real challenge is to
maintain whatever you did."

203
"Indecision is not the same as letting go and letting God."

204
"The rat race is not meant to be run by humans."

205
"The lowest lows of your life will one day break to give
way to your highest highs."

206
"To be or not to be, that really is the question we all have
to answer for ourselves to decide what we choose to
become."

207

"How you feel about life is how life is going to make you feel about you."

208

"This world belongs to the one who can listen without interrupting."

209

"Politics can never be human until the time it is based on extremism fueled by religion, keeps accounts of past prejudices or wages wars when egos clash."

210

"You become a spiritual guru when you begin to love everything and everyone around you."

211

"The world kisses the feet of those who make their own luck."

212

"If you want to stop worrying about money, stop worrying about money."

213
"Like God, some relations are too grand and complex to
be given a name or a label and they are best left
unexplained but never left unexperienced."

214
"Get rid of the burdens from your past or they will get rid
of whatever little sanity that dwells in your brain."

215
"Replace reasons from your life with results."

216
"Most monkeys are better behaved and well-spoken than
most politicians!"

217
"Organized religion is more like organized crime these
days!"

218
"An accident is not caused by the car but the driver
driving it, although a victim is convinced that it was the
car's fault."

219

"Setbacks remind you to stay humble."

220

"You can't solve today's problems with yesterday's solutions."

221

"Listen to the song of your soul, and this whole world will dance with and for you."

222

"Those who don't take full responsibility of their life doom themselves to live a life of mediocrity."

223

"I am not afraid of losing, that's why I always win."

224

"Time is the currency of life."

225

"When you have it, it shows."

226

"All is already well."

227

"As contradictory as it might sound, the quickest way to
lose something is to hold onto it tightly."

228

"Our sole purpose is to fulfill our soul's purpose."

229

"Trust people to trust their instincts."

230

"Words rarely say what many hear."

231

"You cannot escape yourself."

232

"An obsession to relentlessly pursue an addiction sooner
or later destroys the things one loves."

233

"Keep your cool, it's the only thing that's worth keeping
to yourself forever."

234

"Lions are not taught to hunt, they are born knowing it."

235

"Let your children experience the very things that made
you great."

236

"Anything worthwhile that has ever been accomplished
is almost always accomplished alone."

237

"Pain only hurts those who refuse to grow from it."

238

"When you begin to believe that life can be too good to
be true, that's when it will be."

239
"More people than you know care about you more than you think."

240
"Waste your anger only on those who are worth it."

241
"Pay attention or you will pay for the attention not paid."

242
"Real beauty is the cause of demise of everything that crosses its path."

243
"Life's lessons are easily learned but simply forgotten."

244
"Your mind will seek whatever it sees."

245

"One man's stupid mistake is another man's reason for a hearty laugh."

246

"Money might not be everything but it buys almost everything!"

247

"Appreciation attracts appreciation, negativity breeds negativity."

248

"An ugly flower for me might be a beautiful flower for you."

249

"If you are alive, you have permission."

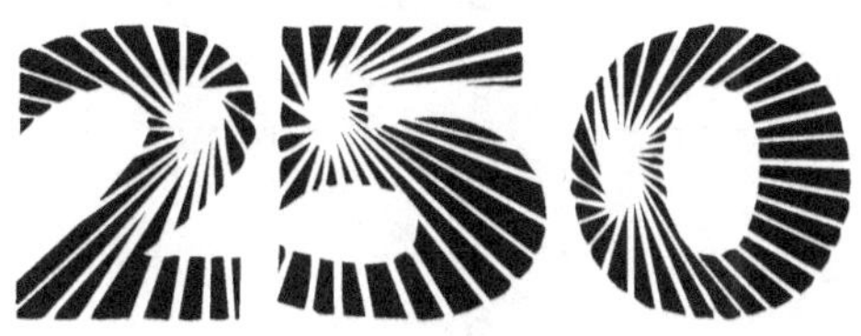

"I choose to believe that God is a She and that's why we refer to nature as 'mother nature' because 'father nature' would've kicked our ass if we ever misbehaved which is something we humans do all the time!"

251

"We cannot keep punishing new generations for the mistakes our forefathers made."

252

"Keep your head in the sky with feet on the ground and not the other way around."

253

"There are no unsuccessful businesses, only poorly marketed enterprises."

254

"Life is about trusting it to work out for you."

255

"You get what you prepare for."

256

"Some people are too smart for their own good."

257

"The positives in life are born out of the negatives."

258

"The power of love speaks no language and yet communicates with all."

259

"Life is all about making stupid mistakes and learning intelligent lessons from them."

260

"Money changes everything."

261

"A man without a purpose sooner or later becomes a pervert."

262

"The lazy of the mind and body are invariably poor."

263

"An unknown best has no power over a known mediocre."

264

"A better life can only manifest from the seeds of problems."

265

"Some ideas are ageless as time itself."

266

"People will only see what they are looking for."

267

"Blame in an unexciting game indulged in by the incompetent."

268

"When someone already has everything needed, that's the time his or her true nature is revealed."

269

"Choose prudence over pride."

270

"Don't just beg to differ, be different!"

271

"I am ______________, and you get to fill in the blank with whatever you choose."

272

"Sometimes the best thing to do is do nothing at all."

273

"Logic plays very little, if any role in a life driven by dreams."

274

"The quality of emotions you feel constantly produces the quality of your life."

275

"Emotions are impervious to logic."

276

"Whatever you feel is a signal to the Universe requesting it to make you feel a bit more of whatever you are feeling."

277
"The hand that gives never remains empty for long."

278
"People can only add to your happiness and not create it for you."

279
"Terrorizing yourself by continuously imagining things going wrong is the most popular and worst time pass ever!"

280
"If you ever want to know what kind of a person you are dealing with, look at her 3 best friends and the company she keeps."

281
"Your success is not dependent on any human but on God."

282
"What goes on inside your mind is your own business."

283

"You cannot make rules for life but you definitely can
and do make rules for your life."

284

"Negativity is like quicksand, the more you struggle
against it the more it will suck you in."

285

"Humans are becoming more like computers, efficient
but inept to think for themselves."

286

"If you are not a part of the solution, you are bound to be
a part of the problem."

287

"We all are rulers of the kingdoms or slums we create out
of our world in our mind."

288

"Being rich or poor is a matter of personal choice, destiny
or fate has nothing to do with it, choose rich."

289

"Wealth, love and health more than anything else are just feelings of the mind, heart and body."

290

"The only thing great about great people is their thinking."

291

"Nobody has their thoughts neither how they feel written on their face."

292

"Choosing not to reply to the crap people throw at you is the best response you can give."

293

"Blaming someone for something you don't have is as effective and smart as sewing a shirt with a damp noodle!"

294

"If your life is not exactly the way you want it to be, it means that you have been procrastinating on taking some decisions that you believe are hard to make."

295
"Love without lust is alcohol without the alcohol in it,
plain as water which doesn't give you a high."

296
"Your life's work is to find something that turns you on
more than sex and then make a living by making a life's
work out of it."

297
"Even if you are bankrupt, you will start to become rich
the very moment you believe you are not poor."

298
"Never be content with what you have in life, but always
be grateful because desire is the elixir of the living and as
soon as you are content, you are as good as dead."

299
"Opportunities don't always come knocking when you
are ready, they barge in when you are in your pajamas!"

"When God gives us hardships to face, there is always a reason which is not known to us at the time we are facing them. It's only later that we are revealed the true nature as to why we went through what we did."

301
"There is at least one person in almost everyone's life that needs to be forgiven before we can claim our bliss."

302
"Hope that human consciousness can rise to a point one day where everyone would be able to do what they really choose to do for themselves and tyranny would be a thing of the past."

303
"Emotions don't require logic, logic follows emotions."

304
"Make your life an extraordinary example that will live on after you die."

305
"Those who truly care for others, dare to choose to do something magnificent with their own lives."

306
"The difference between doing it and trying to do it is the same difference between done and not done."

307
"Everything has an energy signature and when you learn to read it, you can have it."

308
"Love people not for their possessions but for the size of the heart they possess."

309
"See the world through the eyes of the vision that blinds you because only then can the unseen appear out of nowhere to be seen."

310
"Laugh at your own mistakes but be empathetic to the ones committed by others."

311
"Love is what we are made of as well as what we are made for."

312
"The only thing that matters is how you look at things."

313

"Every decision you take comes with a price tag and you stand to decide what you choose to lose or gain from it."

314

"Sex is never the answer to love, but it still is a pretty great answer!"

315

"The only way to live life is to have in it something worth dying for."

316

"Life itself will prepare you for its tests for it is the greatest test of all."

317

"One of the greatest gifts you can give to someone is to inspire desire within them to become greater than they think they are.

318

"I don't know how mean people live their life but it's a horrible lifestyle to begin with."

319
"Shit happens only in life, so when it does, be thankful for the fact that you are still alive!"

320
"Never look behind or at your past, where you are headed is not where you came from."

321
"If you can replicate a person's ideologies, you can replicate their successes or failures."

322
"Nobody knows how stupid or smart you are until you open your trap!"

323
"Your thoughts are like mirrors, they reflect back to you as real life manifestations."

324
"If you ever want to know the truth, look in the eyes of the person saying it."

325
"We all have vices to conquer or make peace with."

326
"You've seen nothing unless you begin to see the divinity inside of everyone."

327
"If you really know what you really want, you will get it anyhow."

328
"The wealthy don't have the luxury of wallowing in self-pity."

329
"Not having it causes you to worry but in truth, worrying causes you to not have it."

330
"Forcing yourself to do the things you don't want done is folly."

331

"The more seriously you take life, the more it will take you for granted."

332

"A secret retains its inherent nature depending upon the ear listening to it."

333

"We all only start living when we start loving."

334

"You cannot commit a mistake from which you cannot redeem yourself."

335

"Great suffering creates even greater leaders."

336

"Having a high willingness to learn is the only required qualification for learning."

337
"Make room for the things you would like to have in your
life and they will come."

338
"Your desires help other's desires to manifest."

339
"There is no life after death, because there is no death,
only life."

340
"A control freak always has more stress than he can
handle."

341
"The only way to become is to be."

342
"It's not a matter of choice but a matter of
consciousness."

343

"I don't worry about my work because I don't have time
to do that when I am working!"

344

"Using foul language sometimes feels so good that it's
fucking therapeutic!"

345

"To be able to take criticism constructively is the apex
quality of personal growth."

346

"Bliss is priceless."

347

"Nobody can plan it better than God."

348

"Wait almost always fans the flames for that which we
are waiting for."

349

"Angels walk the Earth disguised as humans and prefer working behind the scenes, so if you ever came across someone who came out of nowhere in your time of need, you met one of yours."

"Many times, we try our best to make some people, who we hold close to our heart, understand our wonderful ways of thinking, only to be ridiculed by them and to finally realize that we can only change someone who is willing to change themselves."

351

"Children remain emotionally pure of intent because they remain unaware of the diplomacies practiced by the adults around them."

352

"Nothing is BIG or small for the Universe, it is you who decides what you put on the pedestal and what you choose not to."

353

"Love permeates and dissolves the toughest exteriors."

354

"When you treat life right, it's bound to treat you good too."

355

"Happiness attracts more things to be happy for."

356

"Money won't bring you happiness but happiness will bring you money."

357

"Don't indulge in conversations which you feel will brew up any negativity in you."

358

"Life is always magnificent but how we react to it is not."

359

"You can't see your thoughts but you can see their effects."

360

"Love has no reason because love itself is the reason that gives meaning to everything."

361

"Our self is the only thing with which we can save ourselves."

362

"If you are trying too hard, you won't get what you want."

363

"Rather than taking things as they are, see them as you
wish them to be."

364

"Consistency beats almost every other quality required
for winning."

365

"A zero, which doesn't necessarily have value of its own,
when suffixed by a number in your bank account
becomes the source of financial strength."

366

"The truth when repeated often loses its value."

367

"The only thing scarier than failing is succeeding."

368

"May you smile without a reason but never without
meaning."

369
"Being sick gets us the most attention, pity and care from those around us and that's why it is the most indulged sport of the victims."

370
"Just like satisfaction is the death of desire, dissatisfaction is the birth of it."

371
"Compromise is the foundation stone on which the structure of revenge is built."

372
"Even if you are not rich, refrain from being cheap."

373
"May the sacrifices you have made, be the coup de grace to your sorrows."

374
"Life always moves in one direction and so should you, forward."

375
"There is a very thick line between being inspired and a
rip off!"

376
"Every time you go against your intuition will be a time
you'll be sorry."

377
"Life is nothing but experiencing what you have
imagined in your mind."

378
"Everyone likes to live in the illusion that they are better
than the other person."

379
"Whatever was considered impossible a few decades ago,
is child's play today."

380
"Celebrate life's small joys to rope in the bigger ones."

381

"You alone have more control over life than you think."

382

"I don't worry about competition, I just do what I do and raise the bar for myself."

383

"There will be times when you doubt the value of your actions but you must still do them no matter how inconsequential they may seem to you at the time of doing them."

384

"The need to control is the most needed quality to be given up if one has to feel peace."

385

"Following your intuition to manifest something is much like downloading a file from the internet!"

386

"No one can take anything from you, what's yours is yours to keep and experience."

387

"Human beings are intelligent and very intuitive, if you are doing something for someone out of fear or insecurity, your actions will never be rewarded."

388

"Forgive the people who hurt you to a point you don't even remember the reason you needed to forgive them."

389

"A passion for excellence is often wrongly perceived as madness but to some extent, it is."

390

"Agony aunts and uncles perpetuate the very problem they set out to solve."

391

"Disappointments readily and equally fuel failure as well and success."

392

"If you ever raise your hand, do it to give someone something of value in theirs."

393

"Everything you want is already here, it's just a matter of meeting up with it."

394

"Fortunately or unfortunately, life keeps changing."

395

"Anything you want makes you more of who you already are."

396

"Commitment is not something you give to another, the society or the world, it is a promise that you make to yourself and stick by it till the end."

397

"The more successful you become, the lesser you relate to people with whom you used to socialize and the lesser it makes you want to do that!"

398

"Jealousy attracts even more things to be jealous of, learn to love what you are jealous of, to manifest in your life the things that others have."

399

"Life is a unity of paradoxes."

"Your failures will be like funerals, where only the same select few people who are close to you will arrive to give you a sympathetic shoulder to lean on. Your successes however will be like the most happening parties, where even uninvited guests will show up!"

401
"Maintain only those relationships which you can sustain."

402
"Taking responsibility equates to taking back your power."

403
"Just because someone couldn't live their dreams doesn't mean that you can't either."

404
"Be proud of your successes while being humble about them."

405
"Be selfish enough to know what you want from and in your life."

406
"Success requires sacrifice and doesn't fit in the schedule of those who are too busy being lazy."

407

"Having money doesn't solve problems but does solve the problems not having it creates."

408

"The height of a man's character is revealed by the depth or shallowness of his decisions."

409

"The greatest truths are often left undeclared."

410

"From what I have experienced in life, I have come to the conclusion that women are the stronger sex."

411

"We do a lot more work than we are actually supposed to do and that's what ruins everything!"

412

"Love is the simplest answer to all of life's difficulties."

413

"A good deed is rarely forgotten but a bad experience is remembered religiously."

414

"Like a coloring book, the incidents that happen in life are colored by emotions and given meaning to by our perception."

415

"Words cost nothing but sometimes, we all have to pay for them."

416

"When you stop needing what you want in life, it comes."

417

"A victim always attracts to herself a persecutor."

418

"Understanding someone's silence is more important than understanding what they say."

419
"Everything you want is just a few thoughts away."

420
"Success is not handled well by all and thus is not
recommended for everyone."

421
"Give time time to do what you want done."

422
"Saying the right thing at the wrong time gets you
killed."

423
"When you relax and let life take care of itself, it will."

424
"Religion till date has served to segregate us more than
serve us."

425
"Relationships change because they are unable to sustain
change."

426
"Get rid of unnecessary necessities."

427
"Do something about your problems before life forces
you to do so."

428
"Imagine a world where you are paid money to have fun?
Actually, we live in that world."

429
"The most important conversation skill is the ability to
shut up and listen."

430
"No one knows what's in store for us until God opens it!"

431
"The hunger for power is not digested by all."

432
"In life, you get rewarded for being yourself."

433

"Don't spend your time and life on those who refuse to invest in yours."

434

"Things are never as worse as we fabricate them in our minds."

435

"A life without good intentions is lived in tension."

436

"Your heart will always go out to the one who has the power to make you cry."

437

"The truth is far from reality."

438

"As you grow old, replace innocence with compassion rather than cruelty."

439

"You are not a victim of circumstances but rather the inventor of them."

440

"It's better to be a successful pessimist than to be an unsuccessful optimist."

441

"Behind every successful relationship is one that failed."

442

"There are a lot of ways to do something but doing it with love beats them all hands down!"

443

"Wanting something creates more scarcity of the thing you want."

444

"Everything depends on everything."

445

"Fantasies only become reality in life."

446

"When you see a person who is full of shit, you'll see someone who is full of themselves!"

447

"You might not want what you think you do."

448

"Talk is cheap but it's easy to buy into it."

449

"Old hatred doesn't serve new purposes."

"People will never see and would rather prefer not looking at all the sacrifices, blood, sweat and tears at the time of your struggle just to become what you dreamt of becoming. But when you do, everyone wants to know about all the shit you went through to get from where you were to where you are."

451

"When things seem to be happening for the worst,
remember that when we clean our homes, they appear to
have become messier, but in reality, everything is being
rearranged for the greatest good."

452

"Just like you don't entertain a stranger in your home,
protect the abode of your mind from strange thoughts
that might refuse to leave like bad tenants."

453

"Once you become impervious to failures, you won't
have to suffer because of them anymore."

454

"It has always been, is and will always be you against
yourself."

455

"It isn't a coincidence that a dog only bites someone who
is afraid of it."

456

"To grow you must first let go of your need to control everything."

457

"Everyone's life is about sharing their dreams and nightmares with each other."

458

"People will always rise to your expectations no matter how high or low they are."

459

"An excuse is no excuse to excuse yourself from what you want."

460

"One of the surest ways to fail is to try and handle everything alone."

461

"You can't become something that you've been taught to hate or fear."

462

"Be wary and distance yourself from those who make you feel guilty."

463

"Give whatever you want to have more of it in your life."

464

"Setting your goals means not settling for anything less."

465

"It's better to be God loving than God fearing."

466

"Bitching is an expensive sport that'll cost you more than you will ever know."

467

"I am really very happy I have viral fever because earlier I thought it was Malaria!"

468

"Loathing attracts to itself more reasons for you to hate what you loathe."

469
"Don't worry about popular opinions, create them."

470
"That which is invisible has power over the visible."

471
"Success comes in search of those who are too busy giving their best."

472
"A life of discipline is invariably followed by joy."

473
"Aiming higher is a prerequisite to a better life."

474
"Contingencies reveal to us who we are."

475
"It's impossible to do good for someone who doesn't accept his own wellbeing."

476

"You only hate the game when you are losing in it."

477

"Fear can motivate us to great heights and depths."

478

"There is no such thing as an impossible dream."

479

"Life itself is an inspiration to live."

480

"The whole world will become your enemy if you do something against your own will."

481

"No excuse justifies failure and success requires no explanation."

482

"Faith is the act of looking at something that is not there and knowing that it is."

483

"You cannot feel something and not have it manifest in
your reality."

484

"A conscious effort should be made to make every day
the best day of your life."

485

"How you say it matters more than what you say but
means little over what you believe."

486

"When you grow emotionally in your life and people in it
don't, they go."

487

"This world will seldom love you for who you are but for
what you can become."

488

"The demise of negativity is positively inevitable."

489
"Sometimes a family is not the one we are born in but the one we create for ourselves."

490
"Conquering your fears is the most addictive drug which will give you the highest high."

491
"Others can handle your feelings for you as well as a butcher handles meat."

492
"If you don't think I am right for you, I won't be able to prove you wrong."

493
"It's doesn't matter who you are, it's about what I become when I am with you."

494
"It's better to be hated than felt sorry for."

495
"The best teachers are most unconventional."

496
"Life is a song and we live for its music."

497
"True wisdom doesn't argue with itself."

498
"Loss is the grindstone that keeps us sharp."

499
"You are the center of your universe."

"Today is Monday, I won't work as I just don't feel like it. Instead, I am going to wake up late, relax, read a book, go out shopping, listen to some music, jog for a while and just concentrate on feeling good. This is one of the luxuries you have when you are an entrepreneur, the owner of your own companies and are jobless!"

501

"The deepest darkest truth always finds a way to reveal itself."

THE ST★R II

501

Quotes of Love, Life and Truth

DEDICATED TO ALL MY ANCESTORS, ANGELS, FOREFATHERS, GAIA, GOD AND LOVERS, I KNOW YOU LOVE ME. I LOVE YOU TOO.

I dedicate this book to the child within you.
I bow down to the divinity within you. Now let's dance.

"Coincidences and synchronicities are God's way of getting your attention very creatively by any means possible."—Ankush Modawal

We have seen deep into space to discover 170 Billion Galaxies.
There is one Galaxy called The Milky Way, that's where we are.
There are 400 Billion stars in our Galaxy.
We have a Solar System of 1 Star, our Sun and 9 Planets.
We have a Numerical system based on the numerals 1,2,3,4,5,6,7,8 and 9. Also, a 0.
Every Numerical, no matter how big will be made of these 10.
Computer coding is done in Binary language that is 1 or 0.
If you know what that means, we are on the same page.
Coincidence, isn't it?
The plan is grander than you think.
The design is beautiful for it is perfect.
The Love God has for you is greater than you have allowed to feel.
It rises within us as the Mighty Spirits we are.
I get stronger when I feel it within the Temple of my body.
All this is for you and me my love.
Finally, we are talking to each other now.
You were missed, now we meet again my dear old friend. Follow your Goosebumps.

Only the Brave

A puzzle here
you shall greet,
if you can solve
it we shall meet.

Coincidences are cryptic messages from The Prime Creator. They are cryptic for they are meant just for us. They are signs that you must go deeper within yourself alone.

There are Infinite Dimensions of Love in you where our Souls were forged in the name of the Eternal Light by The Prime Creator. The entire Oneverse knows exactly who you are and all your lifetimes. That is our Home. You know it calls you every night. When we sleep, we go back to our Home. We go there when we sleep here. We are the children dreaming there when we wake up here.

We are day dreaming and the stories of our lives are being lovingly read to us by God. Our life is the book that is being lovingly read to us by God. It is the never ending story that the Holy Trinity of us writes together. God is a synonym for destiny.

This is for you. That is why you are here. The One wrote this for you. Enjoy what's here fully, it's yours. It is all just for you.

502

"The first rule of success is to develop a thick skin."

503

"Whatever is happening right now is required to happen
for you to reach where you want to be."

504

"Accept what's coming in your life as pieces of a jigsaw
puzzle, they might not make sense to you right now but
later you'll see how everything fits perfectly in God's
divine design."

505

"A good lesson comes from a not so good experience,
follow your Intuition."

506

"It's a lesson when you pay for your own faults but if you
pay for the mistakes of others, it's a choice."

507

"You can either raise your standards or lower your
expectations."

508

"God always gives you inspirations to your next step, get happy and everything will come to you."

509

"One step in the right direction is worth more than a hundred in the wrong."

510

"When you are unable to make others understand, don't worry, life will teach them that lesson."

511

"I am grateful for your eyes which are reading my words."

512

"Just as we cannot live without breathing, we cannot live without loving ourselves."

513

"It is mankind not man-cruel."

514

"You eventually become like the people you surround yourself with."

515
"When those around you act crazy, shut up, sit back and
pretend you are in a jungle of exotic monkeys."

516
"You are either greatly loved or hated when people start
talking about you in your absence."

517
"The power of a dream always surpasses the strength of
reality."

518
"When going through a tough time, you must gift
yourself the permission to cry like a baby."

519
"Going through Hell is usually the last stop before you
get to Heaven."

520
"Behind every successful man is God's will for him to
succeed, his Queens's love and the surrender to The
Prime Creator."

521
"Stress is the opposite of success."

522

"Hate is an unsophisticated way of loving someone."

523

"Hate is the parent of hurt."

524

"Hurt is the offspring of anger."

525

"You only hate those you love."

526

"Only those who make you happy have the power to make you cry."

527

"If you have ever had your heart broken, you will know the value of a smile because you know how precious tears are."

528

"Our tears come when we need to clean our vision of what we want in life and to make us see things clearer."

529
"I used to believe that my tears are my enemies until I realized that they are my only friends for they are always there with me whether I am sad or happy."

530
"If we ever got anything from crying then we would live happily together, each within our love in our dream home besides the black shimmering exuberant ocean of our tears, and maybe we do."

531
"My definition of a good friend is one who laughs with me in my good times and doesn't laugh at me in my bad ones."

532
"Neither the bad times you wish would go away nor will the moments you wish you could live forever last."

533
"Before we become great at anything, we first must become good human beings."

534
"The important thing in a relationship is not how much you talk but how much you communicate."

535

"The most important relationship you have is with your soul."

536

"When you are happy, God is able to give you more reasons to smile."

537

"Remember that you are dealing with souls who think they are people."

538

"The reason you feel alive when you dream is because God wants you to dream."

539

"Unlike people who listen to what you say, The Universe hears and sees your thoughts and manifests them as your reality."

540

"Attention is the currency of The Universe, whatever we pay our attention to the most is what is attracted to our soul."

541

"When you believe in something enough to know that it is going to happen, it is bound to manifest as your reality."

542

"It's our inherent nature to be humble because nothing is too big for any of us."

543

"Look to The Universe for the things you want instead of expecting it out of people."

544

"The source of all goodness is God, people are like the courier service guy for they just deliver to you what you ordered."

515

"Someone's dream is another's nightmare."

546

"There are no ashes, only wisdom."

547

"Reality eventually always catches up to match your thoughts about it."

548

"You will always attract and keep in your life the essence
of the things that you love or hate deeply."

549

"Keep your faith in whatever is happening is happening
for the best because it is."

"The happiness you feel whenever you appreciate whatever you value means that your soul is seeing through God's eyes."

551
"Happenstance is divine design unfolding itself."

552
"It is the beauty with which you see that lets God reveal
to you things unseen."

553
"You are God's creation and a part of The Divine Design,
there is God within you for you are within God's
creation."

554
"Some truths are bigger than both of us and God desires
our love, just like we desire theirs."

555
"Above all, value yourself for you are a divine part of The
Creative Source, without you, all of Creation would be
incomplete."

556
"Just the fact that you exist means that you are loved by
God because The Creator doesn't make mistakes."

557

"God does things for us that we think are impossible for us to do but there is no stopping the divinity of the light we are."

558

"You cannot run away from your own light self and its grace haunts you, only because life is more beautiful than you were told."

559

"Be humble to all for all is alive and kneels to The Will of The One for it is alive too."

560

"And now all that the eternal almighty has created knows that you know that all is alive and all is love."

561

"The Great Central Sun cares for all those who let themselves be touched by its light."

562

"Your soul clearly knows that there is only One Truth that is God exists and is aware of everything you've been or felt."

563

"You are a human being, not a human doing, being means feeling a thought that comes and feeling calls you to doing."

564

"Miracles happen every day, all day long for those who know in The One's presence when it cannot be seen by their eyes, but can just be felt within their heart."

565

"We go in life to the places where our thoughts saunter the most."

566

"Happy people are lucky people."

567

"Love your life as it is right now and it will become better for you."

568

"Appreciation is the energy which attracts what you want and hate is the energy which attracts what you don't want."

569
"Nothing is mechanical in nature, everything in The Universe is alive for everything you see has a consciousness and always speaks to us as soon as we are willing to listen."

570
"God only reveals things to you when you are ready to own the power in that information of light and integrate it into your own light being."

571
"Before we can do it in this lifetime, it must already be done with love in The Safe Sacred Garden of your Heart."

572
"Nothing in life will make sense until you follow your passion, what you were born to do."

573
"Love is when you can be alone with someone and not feel alone."

574
"Your imagination is the key to setting yourself free."

575

"No other person has the exact same gift as yours."

576

"Fuck the past, make love to your present."

577

"The past is dead, the future is unborn, only the present is alive."

578

"The Universe always fulfills your expectation, the key is to expect what you want as opposed to what you don't want or what you have always got in the past."

579

"God didn't give us the option to live our life in the past or the future because we are meant to live in the moment."

580

"Life tests the amount of faith we have by throwing wicked situations at us in the moments we are in dire need of it."

581

"Life's easy when you understand what it's trying to tell you."

582

"The key to a peaceful mind is to develop the ability to willingly go deaf to unkind words."

583

"Whatever we do in life might seem insignificant to us but it holds a great purpose in The Grand Divine Plan of The Universe."

584

"Silence is the epic and most intricate language of divine love."

585

"The voice of The God within you is heard the loudest in the serenity of silence."

586

"Silence is the language of God"

587

"You've lived an honest moment with yourself if you have been moved to tears by the beauty of love."

588

"There is only one Truth and that is pure love, all other emotions are contained within it."

589

"Disclose your dreams to only those who want to dream them with you."

590

"It takes a lot of strength to be vulnerable."

591

"We are all alike, unique."

592

"No two people love the same way for neither of us are alike and nor are our loves."

593

"I've seen people who don't laugh a lot get their asses whooped by people or life, sooner or later."

594

"I let the world be and make my world what I want it to be."

595
"A seed must leave the comfort of its husk behind before
it can rise to become a tree."

596
"Your dreams are waiting to be lived in the same place
you are afraid to go."

597
"It's best to stay in bed on days you feel that it's a good
day to daydream."

598
"What you wish for others follows you like your own
shadow."

599
"Happiness goes where happiness is."

"Your own love sets you free."

601

"Don't try to explain to others what they haven't yet
physically, mentally or spiritually evolved to
understand."

602

"Solitude is the mirror that reflects back and reveals who
you are to yourself."

603

"Be the one who makes others proud of the very fact that
they know you."

604

"We are connected to our Creator by our emotions, so
our Creator must have deeper emotions as well."

605

"The calmest waters run the deepest."

606

"Your deepest fear is accepting your own magnificence in
the name of Light."

607

"Light devours darkness so your fears are clearly understood and you are always loved even when you are afraid."

608

"Anything that devours darkness is bravura, virtuoso and enigmatic, so it's alright to feel in awe of it."

609

"Life is always changing, sometimes it's painful, sometimes it's beautiful, but most of the time it is both."

610

"Those who are meant to stay will without any reason and those who are supposed to leave will, no matter how good your reasons were."

611

"Your happiness doesn't come from other people but from your own state of heart."

612

"Love is the ultimate predator for it consumes everything that isn't it."

613

"Just the fact that you are alive is reason enough to know that you are worthy to have any and everything you desire."

614

"Know yourself to be right in silence than proving anything else to anyone with words."

615

"Anything that makes you happy is going to attract more happiness in your life."

616

"Always remember that you are an answer to somebody's prayer."

617

"We are connected to God by our emotions and whatever we feel becomes our prayer."

618

"Feel every word you say and you will understand your power."

619

"Life should be simple and full of love for when it is simple, it is full of love."

620

"Life isn't what you live, it is who you become by being in love with everything in it that The Prime Creator has created for us."

621

"Pour all your heart in what your soul guides you to do and everything you ever need will find you."

622

"You don't find a soulmate until you become one yourself."

623

"For those who believe, no explanation is required and for those who doubt, no explanation is sufficient."

624

"Those who are deaf to the whisper of their intuition won't give you any support when you dance to The Song of your Soul."

625

"A person who speaks The Truth might have true
enemies, but has truer friends."

626

"Synchronicity or coincidence is God's favorite language
to communicate with us."

627

"The ultimate affirmation is, I Love You."

628

"Ups and downs come in life because there isn't a place
where you can rise up to if there is no place to fall down
to."

629

"When you do something that you have been delaying,
The Universe surprises you with something awesome."

630

"God stands on the side of truth so whenever you are
truthful, God stands with you."

631

"The worst kinds of lies are the ones you keep telling
yourself that you are not enough."

632

"What seems like a bad thing right now will be the most important thing that can ever happen to you to guide your life towards the path of your dreams."

633

"Just the fact you are a woman makes you beautiful and just the fact you are a man makes you strong."

634

"What you give stays with you."

635

"The ones who test your emotional limits are there in your life so that you may master your own reactions to theirs."

636

"The stories you keep on telling yourself are the ones you eventually end up living."

637

"A smile makes everything even easier."

638

"Let your words be like your silence, very clear."

638

"Expect love beyond words and worlds."

639

"Your heart is always telling you where it needs to be in any moment, all you have to do is follow it."

640

"Follow your heart blindly for it can see into The Divine Light which binds all humanity, all it asks from you is to trust your own magnificence."

641

"The words you speak are an invitation to bring into your life whatever they are about."

642

"The easiest way to make miracles is to know thyself as one with The One within."

643

"When you appreciate what you have, The Universe gives you more to appreciate."

644

"What you love doesn't matter but the very fact that you do, does."

645

"When you give the gift of appreciation to others, you give yourself the gift of life."

646

"Don't torture yourself with another's negativity, you are too precious to this galaxy for that."

647

"The easier you think things are, the easier they will become for you."

648

"Don't try to fix another's life so much so that it fucks up yours."

649

"You begin to fully appreciate the beauty of your life when you start seeing the sunrise and the sunset every day."

"Avoid negativity at all cost because that cost will always be less than the price you'll have to pay later."

651

"You can never make profits while you are counting your losses."

652

"If you are too cheap to invest in yourself, you are already paying a really great price that you can't afford to pay."

653

"Be conscious of what you feed your mind."

654

"Close your eternal eyes, remember yourself, jump knowing that into the locked wall and it will disappear for The God eternal within you."

655

"Where there are trees, there is life."

656

"I know I am serious about something when I laugh thinking about it."

657

"If people have a problem with your opinion, it's their problem, not yours."

658

"Anyone else's opinion of you is limited only to the level of thinking they have and that has absolutely nothing to do with you."

659

"If you aspire to be like someone, just know that there is someone who you inspire to become like you."

660

"Love everyone, reflect only upon yourself."

661

"The judgment anyone passes on you is their own reflection."

662

"Judge no one, for every soldier appears a monster to someone and has himself fought at least one."

663

"Before you can change the situation you are in, you must become happy right now."

664

"One day, the same things and people that have made you cry will make you laugh and the things and people that have made you laugh will make you cry."

665

"The 2nd most powerful 3 words if you mean them are; I forgive you."

666

"Love is to enjoy oneself in the company of others."

667

"Only fools fall in love, the wise rise in it."

668

"You write the story of your life with the pen of your thoughts."

669

"The thoughts you think often and the words you speak become the story of your life."

670

"Love doesn't create dysfunctional relationships, lack of love does."

671

"God made woman the most beautiful and that makes man the luckiest."

672

"Stupidity is the first step into misery and misery is the first step to learning."

673

"It's better to be envied than pitied."

674

"There isn't a wrong time to begin doing the right thing."

675

"Sometimes, the best you can do is cry."

676

"To be desired as much or more by the one you desire is one of the best feelings."

677

"Fear of what you are afraid of manifests what you are afraid of."

678

"Do something special for yourself every day for you are the most important person in your life."

679

"Worrying is the act of putting your faith in what you don't want to experience."

680

"It's great if you have a reason to laugh, it's even better if you don't and still do."

681

"The greatest challenge in life is to be happy with where you are and be grateful for it."

682

"Acts of love are always rewarded."

683

"Always believe in yourself and at times in which you are not able to, believe in God."

684

"Nothing inspires The Divine Masculine form, The Man more than The Divinely chosen Feminine form of The Woman he loves."

685

"A Man is a male who grows up with the child alive within him."

686

"Nothing inspires The Feminine more to express her divine form more than The Man she has surrendered in devotion to."

687

"Own the person that you are."

688

"If you want to be free, you have to give up the luxury of caring what people think about you."

689

"When I praise you, I raise me."

690

"When you start living your dreams, you become an easy target to be criticized by those who are not."

691

"What you truly want to be free of is your opinion of what others think about you."

692

"What others say about you is more telling of how they are rather than who you are."

693

"Only The Love of a Queen makes The Man a King."

694

"A prosperous life for me means loving, giving and forgiving without requiring a reason to do so."

695

"When people you don't know start using your name to get ahead in life, just know that you have achieved something great."

696

"Before you start running your mouth about me, you'd better walk in my shoes first."

697

"A hand that gives never remains empty for long."

698

"You might have a plan but God always has a better design, trust it."

699

"Life is all about having fun, now fun off."

700

"You respect the will of God by paying attention to the coincidences that are flowing in your life and following them."

701

"Love is the most supernatural thing because it is super
and natural."

702

"Life is a dance for those who know how to move to its
music."

703

"The Invincible Invisible Kingdom of Peace rests upon
the foundation of gratitude."

704

"The inner voice is the clearest when you are in
appreciation of The Love which surrounds us all."

705

"Anything that is life changing is powerful and that is
why those who don't understand it are afraid of it."

706

"You only gain the capacity to hate when you are afraid
of misunderstanding something or someone."

707

"Whenever in the process of allowing or release, that is whenever you are breathing in or out, that is always, it is best to be relaxed."

708

"Things happen in life and whatever you take from them is only yours alone."

709

"Being happy for other people's success magnetizes yours to you, it signals The Universe that you are ready."

710

"Before I listen to others, I listen to my head and before I listen to my head, I listen to my heart."

711

"People live imprisoned not in other people's reactions, but in their own reactions to other people's reactions."

712

"The prisoner is The Key, there is no door so it's not locked."

713

"A woman can only understand a man if she understands
his silence and the need to be left alone."

714

"When you say I Love You to someone, mean those
words, otherwise those words are hollow, just like you."

715

"If you are a creative human being, you would know the
peace and inspiration the silence of The Night brings."

716

"Your heart knows deeply the answers to all the
questions your mind comes up with."

717

"Who you really are is felt without you speaking a word."

718

"You are the most important person in your life, only
when you give yourself The Best are you able to give the
gift of yourself to others."

719

"You are God's gift to me and I am God's gift to you."

720
"Being a little crazy in life is like adding a little salt to
food, without it, everything would seem bland."

721
"Creativity to those who don't know it seems craziness
and those who know it, sheer genius."

713
"Success is the shadow that happiness casts."

714
"When you feel happy, you magnetize to yourself things,
people and circumstances that will make you happier."

715
"When someone lies to us, it's for two reasons only,
either they are saving themselves by lying or are saving
you from the truth."

716
"Don't take anyone or anything for granted because they
are the wishes that you were once granted."

717

"I don't care who's with me in my good times, but my
mind keeps a detailed account of those who were by me
in my struggles."

718

"If someone hurt you, give them the BIG F word,
Forgiveness."

719

"The lesson of compassion is often taught by life when it
brings someone to us who we love deeply and must
forgive greatly."

720

"If you ever got to know about other people's problems,
you would realize how blessed you are to have yours."

721

"Nobody can live your life for you because nobody can
think for you and you experience what you think about
the most."

722

"Just like your breath, God is always with you all the
time, even when you don't realize it."

723

"Be quick to apologize and mean it in your heart, no one ever died of being humble so far, it's being too proud that always ends up killing people."

724

"The lack of attention or the presence of it from your man does not equate to the absence or the presence of his love."

725

"Unless you change what you have always thought, you will keep getting what you have always got."

726

"Don't compare yourself to others for you will only arrive at faulty judgment about them and yourself."

727

"This Universe would be incomplete without you, so be yourself."

728

"It is to live our brightest moments that we go through our darkest hours."

729

"Be grateful because somebody, somewhere dreams
about living the life you already live."

730

"To reboot your life, control what you think, look at the
alternatives and delete the negatives."

731

"Speak of The Angel and The Angel appears."

732

"Ask someone who has lost too much and he will tell you
that you don't need much to stay happy."

733

"All religions teach us one thing, love and compassion for
other human beings, and that's all I need to know or care
about."

734

"Two souls in love often get lost in each other to find
themselves."

735

"Arguing with fools doesn't make you or them any wiser,
as they do so only to give themselves an illusion of
smartness."

736

"One thing I learned about fighting is that it's not worth
it."

737

"It is of little importance for others to understand you
but of paramount significance that you understand
yourself."

738

"The world is not changed by those who sit on their asses
but by those who move it and do shit."

739

"When the givers of The Universe start taking back their
power, everything changes."

740

"Every word you say is your command to all of The
Creation in this Universe, so command it well."

741
"Show your fears the pimp hand."

742
"Be lavish in your silence and praises but be meager in
your words and criticism."

743
"If your presence isn't felt your absence won't matter."

744
"Trying to escape change is like running away from your
own shadow."

745
"The only thing you can change about change is your
own reactions."

746
"Live your life in such a way that the legacy of your life
outshines your death."

747
"Those who smile often win hearts easily."

748

"The only way to have a tranquil future is to make peace
in the present with the past."

749

"A grateful heart always attracts more things to be
Grateful for."

"You don't have to be perfect all the time, just be human, that's acceptable and understandable."

751

"Don't attempt to help those who are not ready to help themselves."

752

"Love knows no bounds, if it does, then it is not true love."

753

"It is of the utmost significance to remember the eternal living substance you are made of and be guided from a place of peace, love and happiness."

754

"Love, not hate, makes good things happen."

756

"Develop a taste for life as all the bitter and sweet things we are served in it will one day come to an end."

757

"If you think logically about the existence of anything, you will realize that everything is a miracle."

758

"What you affirm is what you experience."

759

"Those who accept gifts with grace are graced with more gifts."

760

"Your life will never be the same but it can become better."

761

"Don't try to understand the changes in your life, just live them because they will be explained later by life itself."

762

"Your opinion becomes valuable only when it's asked for."

763

"Those who are blinded by anger lose their ability to see things clearly."

764

"Remember those who remember you."

765

"If you've got haters, just know that you've got something that they don't."

766

"All hate comes from those who hold unfulfilled expectations of themselves and want to justify it by blaming others."

767

"If someone gets enough time to discuss you behind your back, know that they haven't got enough productive work to do."

768

"You will never know what you are capable of becoming until the day you lose someone you love the most."

769

"You might not be able to change other people but what you actually want to change is your own destiny."

770

"Everyone cries, only some of us are bold enough not to do so privately."

771

"We were born to dance so let's dance together."

772

"I was born to dance with you, you are reading and I am dancing."

773

"The sooner you realize the fact that you can't please everyone in a given day, the sooner you will stop worrying yourself about it."

774

"Your legacy is etched in you from the past for it has all the answers to your Life."

775

"As you bless, you are blessed."

776

"Make someone's day today, it doesn't matter how little what you do is, it will not be insignificant."

777

"God communicates by giving you impulses and feelings about things as well as people."

778

"The very fact that The Earth spins around The Sun perfectly is reason enough for me to believe in miracles every day."

779

"The people who are a trouble to deal with are those who have trouble dealing with their own emotions."

780

"The Heart doesn't lie about the one it likes."

781

"Hey you, yes you, the one reading this, I just want you to know that you are awesome!"

782

"Whatever you think or speak repeatedly to others or to yourself always has an uncanny ability to come true for you."

783

"Don't get caught up in anything for long that is not on the path of your dreams."

784

"The best relationships are ones in which you don't need to convey your feelings with reassuring words but in which your feelings themselves are strong enough to be silently conveyed."

785

"To hold really strong feelings, you have to be really gentle and humble."

786

"The best memories we end up with are those moments in which we didn't know that we were making memories."

787

"The negatives in your life are attracted by your attention to them."

788

"Your problems will follow you if you turn your back against them but will run away from you when you turn and face them."

789

"Opportunities come disguised knocking on your door wearing a cloak of problems."

790

"All your problems can be solved by thinking differently about them."

791

"The most wonderful idea that anyone can ever discover is the fact that we can and always do steer our lives in the direction of our perception."

792

"Your body is the first thing that responds to your thoughts."

793

"Life is about believing and ultimately knowing that yours is working in your favor."

794

"There are always three who write a story with their perception together, you, me and our Creator."

795

"Ultimately, only you are the best judge of what you are going through."

796

"You will find peace only once you accept your own nature and stop fighting who you really are."

797

"Love, laughter and compassion towards all is our most
natural state of being."

798

"What you see beautifully becomes more beautiful for
you."

799

"You experience your future one second at a time as the
timeless moment of The Eternal Now."

"All the light that you are is with you in this now moment."

801

"The moment you start taking your life seriously, it begins to test your sense of humor."

802

"The best of us are understood the least for elusive invisibility is the greatest power."

803

"Your frustrations don't come as much as from what others couldn't do for you but all from what you couldn't do for yourself."

804

"Only you know what you've seen on the way to reach the place where others see you at."

805

"You are the rock star of your own life because everyone is busy being exactly that in their own."

806

"Men require respect as much as women need love."

807

"Remember that even when you say you don't have a choice, that's a choice."

808

"You have moved on when someone did something that once made you cry, now when you think about it makes you laugh at yourself."

809

"I choose to remain silent on days when words can't justify what I feel."

810

"Your heart beats for a purpose and it has found you."

811

"A genius always keeps his heart open and mouth mostly shut."

812

"Stay far away from assholes who talk crap before they turn your life into shit."

813

"A smile on your face is confirmation that your soul is growing."

814

"Dreamers smile with the people who laugh at them."

815

"As the will to travel is ignited, the path of the voyage is illuminated and appears beneath your feet."

816

"People die from stress, never from chilling out."

817

"If you smile while you meditate, you are doing it right."

818

"You ask The Universe with your feelings and not with your words."

820

"There are no limits to how much we can feel for the deeper the feelings, the more they influence reality."

821

"In the end, the only realization, maybe the regret that remains is that you could have given more love."

822

"The value of a woman can be realized by the simple fact that we all spend the first 9 months of our life in her womb."

823

"Only a man in love can see who she is in the reflection of her tears."

824

"Our emotions are our prayers for our emotions felt within connect us to God."

825

"Dear God, thank you for smacking me in my face when I wasn't listening."

826

"I bow down to God for his will is done through me."

827

"Life gets better for those who believe it's already good for them."

828

"You are alive for a divine reason and only you will know that reason when you look deep within your heart."

829

"You are meant to rise above the everyday bullshit and do epic shit."

830
"Always believe in your dreams, they won't give up on
you until you give up on them."

831
"God isn't challenged by anything and everything we
perceive as problems are just ways to give us a better
experience than what we can imagine."

832
"If you are searching for your savior, go look in a mirror."

833
"Before you can understand another's pain, you first have
to intimately know your own."

834
"Any idea believed in the privacy of one's heart becomes
a reality for the mind that entertains it."

835
"You can only see yourself as good as the mirror you
behold or the camera you hold."

836
"In the Universe, all things are in motion of evolution,
since you are a part of nature, so are you."

837

"The wise often seek divine truths and solace in the all possibilities of silence than in the single possibility of sound."

838

"The best gift you can give to your children and the generations to come is to give them a book you wrote."

839

"When another being is happy because of me, I feel alive because that's life."

840

"Medication can never replace meditation."

841

"In the world of too much talk, silence is often remembered longer."

842

"Sharpen your sword of peace with truth."

843

"Being single doesn't mean you are not loved, it just means that you are not willing to settle for anything less than the best."

844

"You can only see clearly when the light is behind you,
for those who face it directly are blinded by it."

845

"The circumstances you were given, just know that
nobody else could have done it better than you did
because you did your best."

846

"When you keep a clear vision of the future, everything
that is not a part of it fades away."

847

"After you take the first step, everything else flows and
follows."

848

"Through our words, we try to say what our soul speaks."

849

"To be what you want to be, you have to give life the
benefit of the doubt of working for you instead of against
you."

"Your imagination affects what you experience in your reality."

851

"Your life is only as beautiful as you allow your own imagination to believe is possible for everything is."

852

"Before you can get it, you imagine it."

853

"You will get it when you're ready, not when you think you are."

854

"Be your best and let God do the rest."

855

"We always get what we look for and when we look at what we get, we get more of it."

856

"The quicker you plant, the sooner you shall reap."

857

"As you walk your path, you leave a sparkling trail for others to walk theirs as well."

858

"I have yet to see a happy soul who judges others or one who judges and is a happy soul."

859

"Happy people make happy people happier."

860

"Fools make you doubt your own sanity and the wise assure you of its presence."

861

"A good listener is one who listens to what is being spoken, hears what is not being said and heeds why it is being said."

862

"How you handle what comes decides for how long it will stay."

863

"Be secure knowing that whatever's yours, will always be and whatever's not will leave even after your best efforts."

864
"The power of love can only be expressed by those who have experienced it."

865
"You know what your God given gift is when you do it, it makes everything in your life make sense and gives you happiness."

866
"Even the ones you love the most don't deserve the gift of your anger for long."

867
"We are all born knowing our life's calling, it's what you are naturally good at doing."

868
"Personal peace is achieved not through controlling circumstances but by monitoring your own reactions to situations."

869
"When you make it, remember those because of whom you made it."

870

"Nobody can escape the consequences of their thoughts."

871

"The world belongs to those who belong to their dreams."

872

"When it's time to say goodbye, you realize what it meant to stay."

873

"More than anything else, creative people crave for the magical moments of inspiration."

874

"Your only job is to meet or exceed your own expectations, be better today in some way than you were yesterday."

875

"Your work will uplift others once it's something that uplifts you."

876

"No work is great or small for how the Universe guides you to your next step always remains a mysterious adventure."

877

"Smile, God is watching you."

878

"Whenever you look closely, you'll realize that you have everything you need to take the next step."

879

"Don't keep others in the dark because if you do, that's the same darkness that will haunt you."

880

"Radiant health is every living being's natural state."

881

"It's not in my nature to judge people, in my opinion, people judge themselves on the basis of the perception they think others hold of them."

882

"Think thoughts that make you feel warm."

883

"Choose your words wisely for they often become your experience and what you begin experiencing you begin believing."

884

"The easiest way to have what you want is to want what you have."

885

"For a happy life, surround yourself with people who look up to you instead of those who look down upon you."

886

"Like some people, a candle burns so that it can bring light to others."

887

"The moment you begin comparing yourself to another, stop and realize that you are walking on a different path than them."

888

"Make an exception in case of those who are exceptional."

889
"Conserve your energy, refrain from judging."

890
"Your light increases when you see the light in others."

891
"No other person has the luxury or power to define who you are, only your own thoughts and deeds do."

892
"The world becomes beautiful for those who are lost in the beauty of their dreams."

893
"Only love comes naturally and purely to us, the rest is taught."

894
"Nature doesn't hide because it does not lie."

895
"New born animals don't inherit anything else from their parents other than their life and their love."

896

"We all leave everything here when we become one with
the Earth forever."

897

"To be able to see magic in everything is the gift that our
inspiration gives us."

898

"You must listen to your intuition even when other
people ridicule you, life will reward you for it."

899

"If you sometimes think that something's wrong with
you, remember that's not the case, you're just different
from others."

"Out of all the billions of people on Earth, I had the pleasure of meeting you, what a coincidence."

901

"Life changes the very moment you go from thinking
about me to we."

902

"It's better to have real enemies than fake friends."

903

"The Universe recognizes what you think about the most
as your wishes and manifests them in your reality."

904

"Life is literally thought into being, so expect a new day
when you renew your thinking."

905

"Life arranges everything to materialize your deepest
thoughts about your fears and fantasies."

906

"Life's desires consists of only two things, wanting
something to come in it or wanting something to go
away from it."

907

"Love requires no force for it has an eternal power of its
own."

908
"You know that the God within you is alive when hurting someone only ends up hurting you."

909
"Instead of thinking what the other has to offer, cultivate the attitude of what you have to give."

910
"Preference is given on the basis of preciousness."

911
"Don't believe the brilliant excuses you have told yourself, Today is a new moment and you've never been what you have become now."

912
"The price of beauty is attention."

913
"It is better to be left alone rather than have around those who don't believe in you and in the power of your dreams."

914

"Just like you would not be jealous of others if they have what you have, you too can have what you want if you stop being jealous of others having it."

915

"When you play your part, God takes care of the whole."

916

"The next level is always staring you at your face but you don't see it unless your eyes are ready."

917

"When the ancient part of you opens its eyes, it speaks with the softest whisper of love and sends tremors across every particle of the Universe announcing your rise."

918

"The only thing mightier than the human Will is the Will of God imbued within the will of a human being."

919

"Not learning from mistakes is a lot like failing in exams, until you learn what you are meant to, you will have to repeat that class until you pass."

920
"The happiest among us are those who have painstakingly realized that the source of their happiness is within."

921
"Pain is the result of not paying attention when life's trying to teach you something."

922
"You can hang onto hurt or you can hang onto hope but you can't hang onto both because if you do, it'll tear you apart."

923
"Don't focus too much on reality but on what your heart desires and imagine the best outcomes."

924
"Having a pet is like having a child who doesn't speak but expresses everything."

925
"The seeds of love, compassion and kindness bear the sweetest fruits."

926

"There's no way that in any given day you can please everyone and a simple 'no' to others goes a long way for preserving your own joy."

927

"Silence is the language animals use not to talk to us, but to teach us that a whole life can be lived in peaceful love without ever speaking a word."

928

"You can only have as much compassion and understanding for others as much as you have for yourself."

929

"Glitches are just a way of God telling you that there is something better in store for you."

930

"Think more of where you want to be rather than of where you are."

931

"All the light that you are has followed you till this eternal present moment of our Now."

932

"Gratitude comes from the deeply feeling heart, not just the mouth."

933

"Love your life, bad experiences teach you and the good ones make you happy, they both are important."

934

"Be helpful and cheerful because just by being happy, you will be able to give others hope."

935

"Throw the old out manually and the new comes in automatically."

936

"Bad times come in life to see how good you are."

937

"Curiosity and the need to explore the mysteries within your heart is the adventure called Life."

938

"Cooking food for another with love is medicine for your soul and when they eat it, the healing is complete."

939

"Move from an attitude of not because I have to, but because I want to."

940

"Everything you've experienced has evolved you to experience this moment of The Timeless Now."

941

"Whenever you are happy, God is able to guide you the best."

942

"Nature has variety in everything and one that exists never truly has another exactly like it."

943

"Good things are always kept safe because they are infinitely precious."

944

"You evolve by loving the gift of life."

945

"The only thing that can keep me indefinitely entertained is being in nature."

946

"To understand nature is the deepest need of human nature."

947

"Happiness relaxes you and allows yourself to express yourself completely."

948

"I think what I get to experience."

949

"You are the most important person in your life."

950

"The Illusion of coincidence is given to give the illusion of control of one's Destiny."

951

"If you can fall, you can walk, if you can walk, then you can run, if you can run, you can fly."

952

"God is pure love and that energy has always been guiding you in your life, whether you knew it or not, trust that all is well."

953

"Now that you know that God is personally aware of you and is on your side, it will be best to follow your goosebumps."

954

"We are spirits, our emotions connect us to God and when you pray to God, God prays back for you, you get to feel the blessings."

955

"Even the demons bow down to God."

956

"Intelligence is nothing without divine guidance."

957

"If you want the world to be a better place, contribute one good human being to it, yourself."

958

"Your past is the enemy of your present."

959

"What came in the past was on the path."

960

"The path becomes clearer for others as you clear yours."

961

"We all are more dependent on all the cycles of nature than we are lead to believe."

962

"The eye of the storm is quiet and the perfect chaos around it keeps it balanced."

963

"Only a storm leaves the strong behind as stronger."

964
"Life doesn't come with guarantees but with choices."

965
"Trust God to guide your heart for it knows where your body needs to be."

966
"Take my mind to the places my soul would love to go, guide my hands when I do the things I feel in my heart and move my feet to where you think I need to be."

967
"Your soft heart is your power."

968
"The storm in me creates the storm I see."

969
"Live everyday as if it's your birthday for every time you wake up it is."

970
"Just like you feed your body with food, nourish your soul with dance and laughter."

971

"The divine pleasure felt in laughter is because God laughs with us both."

972

"You are never alone in your life, you always have angels and beings of light by your side watching over you."

973

"Dear God, I don't want to ask you for anything because you already know what I want and you give it to me every day."

974

"You are the key to The Universe so much so that how paramount you are in the divine plan has been kept secret from you till now."

975

"The moment you clearly realize your own magnificence, power and brilliance, you will get on your knees, look up at the Heavens and weep with the beautiful realization that God has always been guiding you."

976

"The ones who will cry the most when you die will be those who smiled the most because of you when you were alive."

977

"There is no death as we are eternal and immortal, only our form changes in a never ending cycle of seemingly physical to spirit."

978

"The bitter the truth, the sweeter the person telling it is."

979

"Speak the truth in your heart for those listening might not be used to it but remind them how it feels to be human."

980

"The relationships you have in this lifetime are a reflection of how much love and understanding you have for yourself."

981

"Pain is the sign for you to change your thinking."

982

"In every painful situation, either something needs to be forgotten or someone needs to be forgiven."

983

"Give souls hope for that is what they live on and are alive for."

984

"Your light shines brightest in darkness."

985

"Everything looks more enchanting in the shimmering blackness of the night."

986

"All you need to do to remember who you are is to lift your face and look at the sky."

987

"If you can sit alone in a room for a long period of time and be happy, just know that you are one of the sanest people alive."

988
"The nature within is expressed outside."

989
"When you say I am, God says we are."

990
"It's a divine bittersweet moment when you arrive at the
end of a good book that you were eager to finish."

991
"Sex is a need but a luxury when had with the one you
love."

992
"Only the bravest of warriors go through the toughest of
tests."

993
"We dream of the same faces being by our side whenever
we are in love or war."

994
"Dear God, I just want to thank you in advance because I
know you know me and you'll give me whatever I want,
like you always have."

995

"The greatest love story is yet to be written, for you are still breathing and the best is yet to come."

996

"The key lies in the past, the lock is in the present and the door to the future disappears now."

997

"We are drops of the infinite water for when our time comes, we shall once again be one with the ocean of eternal life, our Home."

998

"When you wake up from sleep, it's a shift of consciousness from the other side of the veil to this one."

999

"The answers you seek in your life are hidden in plain sight waiting to be discovered by you when you simply shift from the matrix on the simpler higher plane of nature to see."

"Human civilization realizes that health is wealth and the human race thinks net worth is self-worth. Your worth can never be measured by money, you are more precious than that. Money isn't even real and we are the only specie on the planet which uses this means of artificial energy for ease of trade. Gaia itself has a consciousness and this free life giving planet itself is alive, just like you are made up of trillions of cells, and you are The Universe or the Single Collective voice of those cells. The real wealth of this planet that is alive is the symbiotic eternal life that lives upon it. Human beings are the only specie on the planet that uses an artificial system of money to exchange energy. Everything else in nature is directly powered from The Sun and grows from within The Earth."

1001
"Your healing will start with self-love."

1002
"The Internet is incomplete and always will be."

170 Billion Galaxies.
400 Billion Stars in our Milky Way galaxy.
The Milky Way galaxy has 400 Billion stars.
I think we are not alone. We never were or will be.
God is with us and within us.
What is possible?

Everything is. Everything is out there.
We are the children of God.
We were born with a piece of God within us.
We have a legacy of cosmic heritage and have a loving family of light bigger than we had imagined.
It is a family of love and light.

We have more star brothers and
sisters than we know of as of now.

They are all one of a kind.
And they keep calling us back to
our home.
All of us are children playing
there.
Let's all dream together one of us
said.
If we fall asleep, the one who
wakes up first will wake up the
others.
We all fell asleep.

We met here.
Only one of us recognized who we
both are.
Wake up now my beautiful friend.
We were the children dreaming
together.

One of us has woken up and is
looking at the other.
Can you feel my eyes on you?
You look so beautiful sleeping that
I don't want to wake you up.
So I waited and I am waiting.

It's a glimpse of Heaven and it's so
beautiful.
I had forgotten to tell you, that
God is playing with us too.
We are within God's loving dream.

Then I whisper in your ear.
You are not alone.
You never were.
You never will be.

Cosmic heritage

"As human beings, we must realize that neither are we above nor below nature but are a part of it. We are one with the plants, the animals, the water, the sunlight and the air. As human beings, we must realize that compassion and love is what makes us humane. Nobody is above nor below any other human as well. Whether you are rich, poor, a negative person, or a positive person, talented or a total slob, when seen through The Eyes of God, we are all equal and thus, that makes us all one."

The fact of life is the fact of light.

Now you have been touched by light and this light is tied to a horse that will never tire.

The key is here.
The lock is gone.
The door doesn't exist.
It's an illusion.

Find me when you wake up.

AND NOW YOU ARE AWAKE.

Ankush Modawal is The Law of Attraction and Feng Shui Practitioner for practical spiritual souls.

Ankush is probably the 1st and ONLY author in the world (to his knowing) to have authored life transformational spiritual self-help titles, quote books and then venture into writing a Dark Comedy Fiction/Reality title; Blue Book.

He has done his schooling from Delhi Public School R.K Puram. Graduation from Delhi University and post-graduation in planning and entrepreneurship from

IIPM. He was awarded as a power achiever of IIPM for Blue Book.

After a series of enigmatic events unfolded in his life and his 3 pilgrimages to the great Himalayas with his then girlfriend, his lifestyle changed dramatically.

Ankush is a new age spiritual author and began his magical journey on the enlightened path that lay before him like it lies before all of us. All you ever need to make your dreams come true is You. This is what he teaches, faith in faith, with faith.

His name and literary contributions are associated with too many people to mention here. He is currently married to his first wife; writing and lives in New Delhi, India.

Feel free to connect with him on Social Networks (@ankushmodawal) and just see what'sup with him!

Black Book One

Genre: Law of Attraction
Released 2008

This is a message from God. Its purpose is to show you how to manifest your dreams that have been eluding you for so long. The change you've been wanting in your life is here. This message is that change.

What you are reading right now is very powerful. If you don't feel the power these words have at the present moment, please turn these pages over. This just means that you are not ready for the message which is in here for you. When the time is right, you will find the Black Books again.

Actually, the first Black Book has found you.

(Hardcover) INDIA ₹749/- US $40 EU €35

The above price includes shipping and delivery cost
WhatsApp <Black Book One> along with your full name and address to +919999993776

Black Book II

Genre: Law of Attraction
Released 2009

Wealth is impartial to us just like the air we breathe. Everything that you want has an energy signature, a kind of a code. Miracles are available to everyone and there is a certain code of conduct which they follow.

But the codes to create them have almost always been left unspoken, until now. You can keep the Black Book II with you only if you resonate with its power. Only if you are finally prepared to live your fantasies.

Otherwise, it will escape and leave you for someone else.

(Hardcover) INDIA ₹ 749/- US $ 40 EU € 35

The above price includes shipping and delivery cost
WhatsApp <Black Book II> along with your full name and address to +919999993776

Blue Book
MBA MaFia Exposed
Genre: Dark Comic Fiction/Reality
Released 2011

To be truthful, this was the end of a dark beginning. I had banished my past in the limbo of my mind and it was supposed to die with me.

But, the deepest darkest truth always finds a way to reveal itself.

A violent struggle of emotions within and a hopeless war with reality to follow an impossible intuition, I secretly wish that this was just a fictional fable, but this is the shocking story of my life.

This is the dark beginning of an end because the truth won.

(Hardcover) INDIA ₹ 749/- US $ 40 EU € 35
The above price includes shipping and delivery cost
WhatsApp <Blue Book> along with your full name and address to +919999993776

Golden rules of the rich & famous for manifesting money

Genre: Law of Attraction/Attracting Money
Released 11.11.2011

Ever wondered why some people have more money than they have use for? What do the rich and powerful do that makes them that way?

Well I found out by real life experiences and from the mouths of the rich and famous themselves. Their secrets have been revealed in this magical book.

(Hardcover) INDIA ₹ 749/- US $ 40 EU € 35

The above price includes shipping and delivery cost
WhatsApp <Gold Book> along with your full name and address to +919999993776

{SMS 2 GOD}
A 1 to 1 with the Universe
Genre: Ask the Universe/Bibliomancy
Released 12.12.2012

How good would it be if you could ask the Universe
questions and get guidance directly from it?

With this book, now you can. Simply write down your
questions, pick a number and voila. There are many ways
to play or read this book. You choose which one suits you
best and leave everything up to the Universe.